nigel risner

You Had Me at Hello

The new rules for better networking

Limitless Publications

Second Edition published in 2004 by
Limitless Publications
Garden House
Garden Close
Arkley Herts EN5 3EW
England

Printed in Great Britain by
Bezir Corporate Print
Poole, Dorset

ISBN: 0-9546836-1-7

Graphic design, branding and marketing support provided by Joanne Bloomfield. For more information visit **www.bsolutions.co.uk**

ACKNOWLEDGMENTS

My everlasting gratitude to:

Fran, my wife, who has encouraged me to be the person I need to be.
As ever you are my rock.

Daniel & Sasha, my two amazing kids who are a constant joy.

Mum & Dad who keep my feet firmly on the ground and network fantastically
on my behalf.

Andrew, my brother, the one person who gives me the feedback
no-one else dares.

Jack Canfield, my coach, mentor, and most importantly, my friend.

Ali my PA who keeps me on the road to do my stuff.

Brian Chernett and Sue Cheshire from the Academy for Chief Executives
who supported me right from the start.

Jennie Harnaman, the brightest young lady I know from the Institute of Sales
and Marketing Management.

Joanne Bloomfield for her help and support with all of my marketing and
product design.

All my friends at the Professional Speakers Association,

Contents

Rehearsal: before entering the room

Performance: In the room

Review: After leaving the room

Dear Reader,

I'd like to tell you the story behind this book. I needed to unwind one evening after a tough day, so I watched the film Jerry McGuire.

There's a scene towards the end where Tom Cruise visits his ex-girl-friend's house, wanting to win her back. He finds the house full of women all complaining about men.

So he launches into a great long speech, explaining how much he loves her. But she interrupts him half way through: "Stop right now. You had me at Hello."

And I thought, how many times when we are communicating with people do we have, or not have them at hello?

I decided to share some insights about how to approach people, make a positive impact, and then engage them in a conversation they will not easily forget.

In the last year I have given approximately 140 speeches sharing these principles and more. I have yet to hear a successful person say that the ideas don't work. Of course I've had my fair share of unsuccessful people who are sceptical about them.

I trust you will find this book interesting. Let me know how you get on.

Happy networking,

Nigel

1

WHY NETWORK?

**The best way to increase your net worth
is to increase your network.**
Nigel Risner

Do you really need to network? Maybe not. If you're happy with the
business you've got and you don't want any more, then possibly you don't
need to network.

In that case, you probably don't need to read this book!

However, if you do want more business than you're currently getting from your
existing clients, friends and so on, you need to increase the number of people
you know. In other words, you need to expand your network.

Networking is a fantastic way to meet new people, share ideas and find out
how you can benefit in a reciprocal manner.

I like to think of networking as an opportunity that allows people to use my
services or to recommend me to someone they know. So I always tell them,
"You may not need a motivational speaker, but I'm sure you know somebody
who might. And the next time you're at a dinner party and someone says they
have a conference coming up and the last speaker wasn't great, you can say:
`Well, I met this guy. I don't know whether he's any good, but here's his card.'
Or something along those lines."

Right now networking is one of the best ways to enhance your business,
because it gives people a chance to buy you. When they meet you and see
how passionate you are about your work, they get a real understanding of
what you're about.

Otherwise, all they can go by is your marketing material. And no matter how brilliant your books are, or your videos and other products, **people want to buy people**. In order for that to happen, they need to meet you personally and see what you're like. Once that's happened, they'll really get it.

The personal meeting is so important that it's worth taking time to think about how you come across to people. If they find you difficult to talk to face-to-face, how will they feel about ordering products from you? The New Rules for Better Networking can help you relate to people in a friendly and positive way and show them that you are a nice person to do business with.

When you consider how little it costs, networking is a phenomenal way of marketing.

But there is one problem. Networking seems unbelievably difficult because we've made it difficult. We think, "Oh no, it's networking. We're going to have to meet people. Help!" We feel that we're being forced to talk, and we don't like that.

Yet really all we're doing is having a conversation with people. What's so hard about that?

When you're going to a dinner party, you don't say, "Oh no, I'm going to have to talk to people." You know that's part of it. If we thought of networking as being much the same thing, it wouldn't seem nearly so difficult.

Networking is one of the best ways to enhance your business, because it gives people a chance to buy you.

There's only one letter different between

n**E**tworking
and
n**O**tworking

the **E** in networking stands for
ENTHUSIASM
and the last 4 letters of enthusiasm
stand for

I
Am
Sold
Myself

2

IT'S OK TO NETWORK

If you come from abundance, you'll get it, but if you come from scarcity you'll get that instead.
Nigel Risner

Before we can network effectively, we need to overcome some barriers in our minds. Many of us have parents who taught us not to talk to strangers. They told us that we need to be on our guard around people we don't know, because they might be dangerous.

That's a bummer if you're in sales!

So one of the first hurdles to tackle is our fear of strangers. We need to reassure ourselves that it's OK to talk to them. Actually, it's more than just OK: it's essential if we want to grow our business!

Just stop and think for a moment. When was the last time you heard of someone being attacked in a networking event? Have you EVER heard of such a thing? I certainly haven't. In all the functions I've been to, I've never heard anyone's security alarm go off because people were doing too much networking. I'm happy to retract my book the first time there's a security scare caused by networking at a meeting of the Institute of Directors, or Business Link. I'll gladly refund the money if the alarm goes off because someone's been endangered by networking.

Many of us have also been taught that our reputation should speak for itself, and that if we're any good people will recommend us. But how would they know? Lots of people, when they meet me, say: "I understand you're really busy." Well, I'm busy - but I'd still like a bit more work.

The best time to network is when you're busy. That way, you won't have quiet periods. There are some people who only network when business is really bad. They're not feeling great because their business is struggling, and then they become desperate. Their anxiety comes across in the way they approach people.

There are literally hundreds of networking events that you can go to.I've listed some useful organisations for you at the back of the book, together with their Head Office telephone numbers to help you get started. These are organisations that hold networking functions on a regular basis, and will be able to tell you about events in your region.

Take this book with you when you go to your first function. Have a quick read before you go into the room. And remember:

- If someone says no, there are only 4 letters you need to know: N-E-X-T.

- They're not rejecting you, they're just rejecting the process.

- Your task is to look for the next opportunity.

We all have a fear of rejection. You might find it helpful to think of fear as Fantasised Experience Appearing Real. Focus on the facts instead.

Whatever your line of business, you know how many people you have to contact to make a sale. For example, if you expect to sell to 1 person in 10, and your commission is £100, every time someone says No, you can thank them for earning you £10. We get hung up on the 1 meeting in 10 where we get the order. But in fact every meeting is worthwhile because it moves us that much closer to the goal. And of course there's no way of knowing which meeting is going to lead to a sale.

So I always say thank you to everyone I meet, because each conversation is worth something to me - they're all part of the process of making my next sale.

The more you practice networking the better your success rate becomes. So you may find that instead of a 1 in 10 ratio you start achieving 3 in 20. When that happened to me it made me want to go out and meet as many people as possible.

It's a numbers game, and savvy networkers play to win.

The best time to network is when you're busy. That way, you won't have quiet periods.

3
BOOST YOUR CONFIDENCE

**Don't be afraid of the space between your dreams
and reality. If you can dream it, you can make it so.**
Belva Davis

There are many books on networking. But all the research shows that
self-esteem, or the lack of it, is the No. 1 reason why networking is a no-no
to so many people.

The more confident you are, the more you'll enjoy networking, and the more
you'll get out of each event. In networking, as in so much of life, a lack of
confidence can really hold you back.

The first part of this chapter provides some practical tips for boosting your
confidence when preparing for your next networking opportunity. In the second
part of the chapter I discuss self-confidence in general and suggest some
ways that you can become a more confident person in every aspect of your life.

PART 1:   Boosting your self-esteem before the next
networking event.

Think about where you are, where you come from, and where you're
going - and how this networking opportunity will help you to get there.

Acknowledge the positive past by making a list of all the successes you've
had so far. Keep adding to this list, and read it whenever you need a
boost - e.g. just before the networking function!

Beware of the trap that catches 99% of us: comparing ourselves with people
who do a specific thing better than we do. When I was playing professional

tennis, my hero was Jimmy Connors. It was very unlikely that I would ever be able to play as well as him. But then one day I read in a magazine that the ONE thing he wanted was to have a happy, stable relationship. I'd just met my wife, Fran, at the time. Imagine how I felt when I realised that I had the one thing that Jimmy Connors wanted - a happy, stable relationship. My self-esteem suddenly increased! There's a lovely line that says, "Compare all of you to all of them, and then you may find you're not doing so badly."

Talk to yourself in positive, supportive terms. Princess Diana once said, "If I spoke to my friends the way I speak to myself, I wouldn't have any friends." Most of the time we're unbelievably negative when we speak to ourselves: we focus on what we can't do, and what won't work. And the results speak for themselves. As the quote says, "Whether you think you can or you think you can't, you're probably right."

The past is a place of reference, not a place of residency.

Most of us have had messages in the past that tell us that we're not good enough. So begin to redress the balance by identifying your strengths. When you know what your strengths are and you work from them, things change. Carl Rogers, an eminent therapist said, "What I am is good enough, if only I would be it openly."

Spend as much time as you can with people who support you in your work and your dreams. Ask them to tell you what strengths they see in you, and to give you feedback about developing these strengths. This is so important that I've written a book about it: **"I want, I want...let's get" The New Rules for Better Goal Setting.**

Use the power of visualisation as you prepare to network. Imagine yourself enjoying the event, standing confidently, smiling at people and learning interesting and valuable information that will help your business grow.

Part 2: Building your self-confidence for the longer term

A young woman wrote to me recently about a dramatic change in her level of confidence. She told me that her whole life had taken a different turn since hearing me ask the question, "What one great thing would you do if you knew you could not fail?"

This was a question she had never dared to consider before - but now she could think of nothing else! She had come to realise, in a great, blinding flash of clarity, that the main thing separating her from her hopes and dreams was a lack of belief in her own ability.

This young woman is not at all unusual. Most of us are like this for most of our lives. There are many things that we want to be and have and do, but we hold back. We're not sure that we have what it takes. And because of this lack of confidence, we seldom step out in faith in the direction of our dreams.

Abraham Maslow said that the story of the human race is the story of men and women "selling themselves short". Alfred Adler, the great psychotherapist, said that men and women have a natural tendency to feel inferior and inadequate. Because we lack confidence, we don't think we can do the kind of things that other people have done. And in many cases, we don't even try.

Many of us believe that we're not good enough to succeed. But notice that in the middle of the word BELIEVE are the letters L-I-E. The notion the you're not good enough is a lie.

Just think about these questions:

What difference would it make in your life if you had an absolutely unshakeable confidence in your ability to achieve anything you really put your mind to?

What would you want and wish and hope for?

What would you dare to dream if you believed in yourself with such deep conviction that you had no fears of failure whatsoever?

No matter how low your confidence is right now, it IS possible to raise it. If you follow the example of confident men and women, your feelings and results will begin to match theirs.

The key is to be true to yourself. This means focusing on the very best that is in you, and living your life in harmony with your highest values and aspirations.

Take some time right now to consider these questions:

Who are you?

What do you believe in?

What is most important in your life?

Now decide that you'll never compromise your integrity by trying to be or say or feel something that isn't true for you. Have the courage to accept yourself as you really are - not as you might be, or as someone else thinks you should be. Tell yourself that, all things considered, you're a pretty good person.

Each one of us is an extraordinary individual with a unique blend of talents, skills and abilities. No one, including yourself, has any idea of your capabilities, or of your future potential. Perhaps the hardest thing to do in life is to accept how extraordinary you really can be, and then to build this awareness into your attitude and personality.

Self-esteem is an important starting point, but it isn't enough. People have tried positive thinking and wishing and hoping for years, with only mixed results. What we need is positive knowing, not just positive thinking.

Lasting self-confidence comes from a sense of control.

When you feel in control of yourself and your life, you feel confident enough to do and say the things that are consistent with your highest values. Psychologists today agree that a feeling of being "out of control" is the primary reason for stress and negativity and for feelings of inferiority and low self-confidence.

The best way to get a solid sense of control over every part of your life is to set specific goals. This will give you a clear sense of purpose and direction.

Being true to yourself means knowing exactly what you want, and making a plan to achieve it. Lasting self-confidence comes when you know that you have what it takes to get from where you are now to wherever you want to go. You are behind the steering wheel of your life. You are the architect of your destiny and the master of your fate.

Instead of being preoccupied with the fear of failure and loss, as most people are, you'll focus on the opportunity and the possible gains of achievement. With a clearly defined path ahead, you'll become success-oriented. Gradually your level of confidence will build up to the stage where you can take on whatever you want.

Become very good at what you do.

Another essential way to build your self-confidence through positive knowing rather than just positive thinking, is to become very good at what you do. The flip side of self-confidence is self-efficacy: the ability to perform effectively in your chosen area.

You can raise your confidence instantly by the simple act of committing yourself to becoming excellent in your chosen field. This instantly separates you from the average person who drifts from job to job and settles for mediocrity.

Some years ago, a young man named Tim came to one of my Personal Development seminars. He was shy and introverted. His handshake was weak and he had tremendous difficulty making eye contact. He sat in the back of the seminar room with his head down, taking notes. He seemed to have very few friends, and he didn't socialise much during the breaks.

At the end of the seminar he told me that he was in sales and hadn't been doing very well. But he had resolved to change, to go to work on himself, to overcome his shyness and to become very good at selling for his company. He then said goodbye, and I wished him the best of luck as he went on his way.

A year later he came back to take the seminar again. But this time there were some distinct differences. He was calmer and more self-assured. He was still a little shy, but when he shook hands his grip was firmer, and his eye contact was better. He sat toward the middle of the seminar room, and he interacted quietly with people around him. At the end of the seminar, he told me that he was starting to move up in his sales force and had had his best year ever. He was determined to do even better in the year to come.

About 14 months later, Tim was back.

This time he brought five people from his company, all of whom he had persuaded to take the seminar, and he had offered to pay their tuition if they weren't satisfied. He walked right up to me and shook hands firmly, looking me straight in the eye with a strong, self-confident smile. He asked if I remembered him, and I told him that I remembered him very well. He said that he had brought something to show me.

He pulled out a letter from the CEO of a national corporation - one of the biggest companies in the country - personally congratulating him on the outstanding job he had done in sales during the past year.

It turned out that Tim had gone from No. 33 to No. 1 out of 42 sales-people. His income had risen from £26,000 a year to £98,000, and he had increased his sales volume faster than any other salesperson in the country.

He was still quiet, but he had a wonderful air of power and purposefulness about him. He had taken the steps and paid the price to build himself into a fine young man. He had made the decision to do whatever was necessary to overcome his shyness and to develop the kind of personality that he admired in others. He was, and is, in every sense of the word, a self-made man.

Two laws that affect your interactions with people.

Perhaps the most wonderful result of developing high levels of self-confidence is the positive impact that your personality will have on your relationships. There are two laws that determine much of what happens to you in your interactions with people.

1. The law of attraction, which says that people who are very much like you will inevitably be drawn into your life.

2. The law of correspondence, which says that your outer world of relationships will correspond, like a mirror image, to your inner world of personality and temperament.

Taken together, these laws say that as you change in a positive direction, you'll find yourself surrounded by people who are very much like the new person you are becoming. As you get better, the quality and quantity of your relationships will get better. You'll meet more positive, interesting and self-confident people. You'll find yourself getting on better with members of the opposite sex, including your spouse. You'll find yourself doing better at your job, or even holding a new job, and getting on better with your boss and your colleagues.

Your attitude of confidence and calm assurance will make you more attractive to people. They will want to be around you, to open doors for you, to make opportunities available to you that would not have arisen when you didn't feel as good about yourself as you do now.

Often, people lack self-confidence in their relationships with others because they feel inferior to them. It's easy to become self-conscious of what you're doing and saying, and to be afraid that people won't like or accept you as you are.

But remember:

No one can affect your thoughts or feelings unless you want or expect something from them.

So the secret is to practice detachment. Once you've decided in your own mind that you don't want or expect anything from the other person, you'll find that they can't shake your confidence nearly as much as before. The people who have the best relationships have a calm, healthy detachment from others. Although they're friendly and like to get involved, they don't allow other people's behaviour to determine how they think and feel about themselves.

It's our fears and doubts, more than anything else, that undermine our self-esteem and confidence, pulling us into negative thoughts about ourselves and our potential. As Maslow said, we begin to "sell ourselves short" and see all the reasons why something might not be possible for us. We magnify the difficulties and minimise the opportunities. We become preoccupied with the possible losses we might suffer and the possible criticisms we might endure. Our fears and doubts paralyse us, preventing us from acting boldly, lowering our confidence and giving us a pessimistic outlook.

Most people are so busy being afraid that they hardly have time for anything else. If you don't believe me, just watch and listen to them for a while!

Learn to use this sure-fire cure for negative emotions

The only real antidote to doubt, worry, fear and all the other negative emotions that sabotage our self-confidence is action. Your conscious mind can only hold one thought at a time, whether positive or negative. When you're busy and purposeful, stretching your abilities as far as you can, positive feelings will surface - and you'll start feeling more confident.

Act as though you couldn't fail. Act as though you were already confident. And keep asking yourself: "What one great thing would I dare to achieve if I knew I could not fail?"

Whatever your answer, you can have it - as long as you can dream it, and develop the confidence to go out and get it.

4
FIRST IMPACT

**The difference between ordinary
and extraordinary is that little extra.**
Jimmy Johnson

From the moment you walk into a room, you are making an impact. During your first 30 seconds in the room, people will be watching you, judging you, and wondering what you'd be like to work with. It's absolutely vital that you understand this and are prepared for it. The effect on your business either way could be enormous.

I've used this quote before, but I think it's worth repeating here:

"If you think you're too small to make an impact, try going to bed with a mosquito in the room."

In order to create a good first impression at a networking event, you need two things: preparation and confidence. Of course, these are very closely related. The better prepared you are for networking events, the more confident you'll feel - and the more smoothly everything will go.

So spend time in front of your mirror. Practice what to do and say during those vital 30 seconds until you've got it right. Get feedback from your family and friends.

Think about what message to convey through your body language, including the clothes you wear! A woman rang me up after a networking event and asked: "Do you remember me?"

"No," I replied.

"I was the tart in the red dress."

"Now I remember you."

Make yourself memorable

There's a lot that you can do to make your appearance memorable. One woman I know wears a hat to every networking function she goes to. That way, everybody knows when she's entered the room! If hats or crazy bow-ties don't appeal to you, think about some other way that you can help people to remember who you are.

There's a picture of me on my business cards, my website, my postcards and the back of every book I write. It shows me there, "in your face", because that's where I want to be, asking people questions and making them think. I'm the rottweiler of self-esteem and personal development. People know my stance: I don't let go.

When networking, your aim is to make such an impact that people "get" you by the time you first say hello.

But what if you're not very confident right now? In that case, I suggest you take something with you that's fun. I've been working recently with a company that makes furniture. We've shown them how to make a business card out of wood.

That's just one example. If you've got a chair or you're into music, you could do something that represents your business. It could be a musical tie, or an invitation, or a little toy or gadget that you give people as a reminder. Just something that's a little bit different to what everybody else has got. The greater the impact you can make at first, the easier your conversations will be.

I recently met a man who always carries four apples with him. When people ask him why, he launches into his introduction. His work has nothing to do with apples, but they're a great way to get the conversation going.

We'll talk about what to say (your 'elevator speech') in Chapter 7. All you need to start the ball rolling is a sound-byte: something that's very quick to say, and that trips off the tongue. It tells people what you can do for THEM. Once you've prepared and practiced this introduction, it will come out quite naturally when people ask what it is that you do.

When people ask me, I've got a couple of statements ready. I'll often tell them, "I turn limited people limitless. I take people from exhaustion to exhilaration."

Knowing what to say ahead of time gives me lots of confidence when meeting new people.

I don't need to waste any energy thinking about it, or wondering how it will sound. It's all there, ready for me.

The secret of your first impact is very simple:

Walk into the room, knowing that you've got something important that's worth sharing.

Once you're in the room, use body language to your advantage:

- Walk tall.
- Maintain eye contact.
- Show an interest in what's going on.
- And do something really scary: smile.

Yes, it's OK to smile. Many of us have the idea that because networking is so important, we've got to be really serious about it. BUT WE DON'T! There are a lot of other frightened rabbits in the room, and it's OK to smile.

Enthusiasm and passion will attract people to you.

Remember: most other people at networking events are as just scared as you. The result is a room with 400 people in it, all feeling too scared to circulate and meet new people.

I have a great cartoon in my office. It shows lots of people with their backs to the wall, talking to the same person they came in with, while all the tables and chairs in the room are empty. All these people are talking to the people they already know and thinking they'll get more business.

But they won't!

Of course it's easier to talk to the people we know. It feels familiar and safe. But how will that generate more business for anyone?

It's natural to be afraid of the unknown. But do you want your business to suffer because of it?

5
BE A HOST

People of accomplishment rarely sit back and let things happen to them. They go out and happen to things.

Elinor Smith

One of my golden rules for networking is to be a host of the party, not a guest. And one of the best ways to do that is to offer to help out, either with name badges or to go and meet and greet some people because the host's job is to meet as many people as possible and to make them welcome.

When we act as a guest of the party, we tend to wait for people to come and see us.

But as a host, your role is quite different. My suggestion is that you try to meet between 5 and 30 new people at each networking event you attend. Go up to them and say, "Hello. How are you? Good to see you here. How did you get here?" Just ask them general questions as if you were the host, putting them at their ease and helping them to get warmed up. Don't go into business talk at this early stage.

I suggest that you act as the host for as long as you can, and meet as many people as possible. It will help you to relax and get into the mood for networking. It will also give you lots of useful information about a great variety of people. This will pave the way for the business conversations that you'll have later on.

It takes tact and finesse to be a good host. Here are a couple of pitfalls to avoid:

1. Avoid being over the top. There's a lovely line that says, "Don't think less of yourself, just think of yourself less often." Being a host is about having high self-esteem and walking into the room with passion, but not walking in like John Wayne.

2. Avoid name badges with long names on them, as they'll just put people off. If your name is long or difficult in any way, people will have trouble reading it, and the organisers will probably spell it wrong anyway. So when you go to a networking event, ask them to put your first name in bold letters on the badge. My name badge comes with me wherever I go. It just says Nigel, and underneath that: Turning limited people limitless. I've found most people have no idea how to spell Risner, or even pronounce it, so it's best to leave it out.

Be proactive, help other people feel at ease, help them get something useful from the event, and you'll be surprised how much more you get in return.

6

MEET NEW PEOPLE

If you keep doing what you've always done, you'll keep getting what you've always got.

Stephen R. Covey

One of the things I see many people do at networking events is to come into the room and stand with their backs to the wall, hoping the wall needs some support, and they kind of hold on to it. Well, I'm going to tell you now: no wall in any building that I've ever gone into needs more support.

And then while they're stuck to the wall up comes this magical periscope and they start looking for people they already know, because that makes them feel comfortable.

The problem with this approach is that if you spend time with the people you already know, you'll probably just do more business with them. That's great, but if you want to attract more business you need to start meeting some new people.

How to start a conversation.

I suggest that you look around for people who look lonely and miserable and may not want to be there any more than you do. You could make a joke such as: "Don't you just hate coming to places like this, where you don't know anybody?" That will help the other person to feel a little more comfortable, and you'll have some common ground.

Spend a few minutes with lots of people.

It's important not to spend too long with any one person. In the very beginning when we're feeling uncomfortable because we don't know anybody, we tend to look for somebody familiar - or wait for somebody to come up to us.

Then what happens is that we become very comfortable being comfortable and so we end up talking for 20, 30 or even 40 minutes talking to one person when there's a whole plethora of people in the room that we could go and meet.

To avoid falling in this trap, my suggestion is that you spend no longer than 7 minutes with any one person.

How to end a conversation.

Now comes the question of how to end that conversation and move on to a new one. I suggest that you take this person and introduce them to someone else in the room. This gives you the perfect opportunity to go and find someone else to talk to. Remember that your objective is to meet lots of different people in order to broaden your network of contacts.

Of course, at some point you're likely to find someone really interesting. When that happens, make the most of your time together and try to get to know them. Ask the usual questions to draw them out about their work: Who ... ? What ...? Why ...? Where ...? What do you sell? Where are you based? Who are some of your main suppliers? Why do you do what you do? Why do customers keep coming back to you? These are questions which people will answer with anything but a Yes or No answer.

Then after about 7 minutes with this person, bring the conversation to a comfortable close by saying, "I'm really pleased to have met you. Let me introduce you to someone else who may also benefit from your services." And if you've been in the room and have been listening carefully, you can now extend the "host" role you had earlier by taking this person to the next group of people and saying: "I've just met John and I think he'd be perfect for some of the things that you may need." Or you could say, "Can I introduce John. He's an accountant with some really creative solutions to help you maximise your returns."

Now that you've done the introduction, you can move on and find some other new people to talk to.

Group networking

People often like to go to a networking event with colleagues or friends. Sometimes you see these packs arriving - a whole group of people from the same company, all wearing their company badges and talking to each other. Not only is this not good for finding new business, but it can give staff the mistaken idea that they are here just to have a party.

If you must attend with a group of colleagues, I suggest that instead of hunting in a pack you split up and agree to meet every half hour or so.

The only time I would recommend that you network with someone is to go to an event with a friend from a different organisation. Then you can be each other's PR machine and introduce each other by saying:

"Can I introduce Peter, who's fantastic at ..."

One of the greatest gifts you can give to anyone is the gift of attention.

Jim Rohn

7

YOUR ELEVATOR SPEECH

**It's better to be prepared for an opportunity and not
have one than have the opportunity and not be prepared.**
Whitney Young

As you circulate and meet people at the networking event, sooner or later
somebody will ask you about your work. The best way to answer this is with a
sound-byte: a short, simple statement that shares a message about what you
do and how this benefits your client.

This is known as your elevator speech because it's short enough to be
delivered while you're in an elevator, travelling from one floor to the next.

In order to be really effective, your elevator speech needs to focus on your listener, not on you.

Most people, when I ask them what they do, will spend a minute or so telling
me what they don't do. Or they'll tell me they're from a large family firm based
in the North, or based in the South, with 300 staff. Or it's a small family firm.

The truth is, none of that is relevant to me. What I'm interested in is what
they can do for me. So I would urge every single person whoever goes to
a networking event to think about a sound-byte that briefly describes what
they do.

Whenever anybody asks me what I do, I don't think there's much value in
saying, "I'm a motivational speaker." What I've now learned is to have a couple
of sound-bytes. When someone asks what I do, I'll often say, "I turn limited

people limitless. I take people from exhaustion to exhilaration."

There are many ways that you can express what it is that you do for your clients and customers, whether you're a coach, or a business manager, or an accountant. Here are some examples:

"Our aim is to make your business more profitable by reducing your taxes."

"Our aim is to increase your investments by finding the appropriate place to safeguard your future."

"We sell dream homes. We allow you to live in the comfort you've always wanted to be in."

The secret is to ask what it is that you do for your client or customer, as opposed to what you sell.

Nobody ever bought a chair just for the sake of having a chair. The reason they bought a chair is in order to be comfortable in the surroundings they need to be in. So if you're into furniture, my suggestion is to tell people: "We allow people to have the best experience of their lives while watching television." Now that's the same as saying, "I sell chairs."

Or is it? Think about the impact of the two sound-bytes on your listener. Which is more likely to pique their interest and keep the conversation going?

If you want to make the most of networking opportunities, you need to have your sound-byte or `elevator speech' prepared. And it needs to be so short and intriguing that it opens doors. When people hear it, they automatically want to find out more.

An elevator speech enables you to introduce yourself and your services to new contacts. But it's also perfect for any other occasion when you're talking to people who might be interested in what you have to offer them. As such, it forms an essential part of your networking strategy.

A great elevator speech has certain characteristics:

- It comes across naturally
- It sounds like you
- It takes less than 10 seconds to deliver
- It gets straight to the point
- It briefly describes what you do and how this benefits your clients
- It makes your listener want to find out more
- It opens out the conversation

Unfortunately, it's much easier to introduce yourself in ways that don't achieve the results you want. Have a look at these introductions which don't lead anywhere in particular:

"Hi, I'm Liz. I do sales training."

"Great to meet you. My name is Jo and I'm with a local accountancy firm."

"Hello, I'm Chris. I'm an IT consultant."

Because these introductions say nothing about benefits and value for the client, they don't open the conversation out and so, in networking terms, they achieve very little.

However, with a bit of tweaking, they could become much more effective. It wouldn't be hard at all for Liz, Jo and Chris to turn their introductions into great elevator speeches.

Instead of telling people that she's a sales trainer, Liz could say:
"I help companies to boost their profits by closing more sales."

There's no need for Jo to mention accountancy at all. Just saying
"I help companies to pay less tax" will capture his listeners' attention!

And Chris the IT consultant could say something along these lines:
"My company helps people save time and money by using the best computer software to suit their needs."

Questions to ask yourself when preparing your elevator speech

- What do my clients really need?
- How does my company meet their needs?
- Do I give them great value for money? In what way?
- What practical benefits does my company offer?
- How do my services improve my clients' lives and work?
- What makes my services unique?

A great elevator speech grabs your listeners' attention and stimulates questions. If your speech focuses on them and how your company can help them reach their goals or improve their lives in some way, they're much more likely to stay interested.

On the other hand, if you talk about yourself they're likely to switch off. As a result, you could miss out on all sorts of new business opportunities.

So, when preparing your elevator speech, try saying what your company does, and then ask yourself "So what?" This will help you focus on the benefits that your clients get from your company.

Imagine that a man you meet at a networking event has a problem that you could solve, but your introduction focuses on who you are, and not on how you can help him. As a result, he never finds out how your services could benefit his business! What a waste all round.

The secret is to drive the conversation forward by focusing on the value and benefits you offer, and by asking questions about the other person's business. That way you're more likely to find out if they need something that you can supply.

A great elevator speech buys you a little more time with that person - and that can make all the difference.

Remember: your goal is not to talk about yourself and what you do, but to find out about other people - who they are, what line of business they're in, and what matters to them. If your services are relevant to their needs, they'll almost certainly want to find out more.

Less is more

You could have an elevator speech of 20 seconds, or 30-45 seconds, as some people recommend. But I think the shorter it is, the better. Under 10 seconds is ideal.

The purpose of you elevator speech isn't to tell the other person all about who you are and what you do, or how long you've been in this line of work - especially at the start of a conversation. Your aim is to capture their interest and open the conversation out.

By asking questions about the other person, you're buying time in tiny increments. You're making the conversation worthwhile to the other person, and stimulating them to keep talking to you about their life and their business. The more interested and involved they are in the conversation, the more you'll learn about them, and the better this could be for your business.

In an odd kind of way, your elevator speech isn't really about you at all. Its main focus is on the value and benefits that your clients gain from dealing with you. It's about the practical ways in which their lives and businesses are enhanced by the services you offer.

You may want to develop different elevator speeches for use on different occasions and in different contexts. Who you're talking to, and why, can influence what you say about your services.

The secret is to hook your listener's attention and keep it as long as you can.

Writing your elevator speech

This will take some time, but it'll be time well spent. Think of it as an investment that will give you huge returns. Think too of all the situations where your elevator speech (or a slight variation of it) can enhance your business. It's a great networking tool, but it can also be used whenever you're contacting people, whether by phone, mail or email. If you like, you can put it on your business stationery and in any marketing material that you send out.

1. In order to write the best possible elevator speech, you need to generate masses of ideas. So I suggest that you take a piece of paper and do some brainstorming - either by yourself or with someone whom you trust and who understands your goals.

2. Write down all the things that you do for your clients - in other words, how do your clients benefit from your products and services? Let your mind roam freely. Don't worry about organising any of the ideas at this stage. Just jot them down as they come to you, no matter how bizarre they may be. Some of the ideas will overlap, but that's OK. Write them all down. This is a creative process, so go with the flow.

3. Next, think about the reasons why people do business with you. Do your products and services improve people's health, relationships, productivity, profits, fitness, etc? Using another piece of paper, write down all the ideas you have in response to this question. As before, don't worry about overlap or organisation: just brainstorm and write.

4. Once you've stopped brainstorming, keep the lists on your desk or somewhere handy so you can add to them as ideas come to you later-in the shower or wherever!

5. Look at the ideas you've written down and choose the ones that are most likely to stimulate conversation when you meet someone.

6. Work with them, making sure that the words are non-threatening to the listener.

7. You may find it helpful to develop your elevator speech in two parts. The first part could describe what you do, and the second part could describe the value and benefits this offers the client. For instance, "I help people design and landscape their gardens so that they can enjoy them all year round with minimal fuss."

8. Now take a fresh piece of paper and write your elevator speech out. Once again, leave it somewhere prominent so you can play with it over the next few days. Experiment with the words, changing the sequence, substituting other words that have more energy, etc. Does it get your key ideas across? Does it stimulate interest and conversation? Say it out loud and listen to the rhythm. Is it easy to say? Does it trip off your tongue? Above all, does it sound like YOU?

9. If variations occur to you, write them down as well and fine tune them in the same way. Some people find it's handy to have several elevator speeches ready for different contexts. But I suggest that you make sure all of them are less than 10 seconds long.

10. Next, practice your elevator speech out loud, standing in front of the mirror. Go through it over and over again until it sounds perfectly natural and comes across with sincerity and passion.

With a great elevator speech prepared, you'll feel much more confident next time you meet someone new. Your networking skills will grow, and so will your business.

8
BUSINESS CARDS

First impressions count!

Make sure you have your business card handy at a networking event. Often people will want some information about who you are, and the worst thing to do is to say, "Oh, I haven't got my business card. Tell you what, give me one of yours and maybe I'll call you." And then they can't find theirs!

The best thing to do is to have your business cards in a smart wallet or card-holder. I have a rolodex so I can roll out a fresh, clean business card whenever people want one. That way it's done professionally.

If you keep your cards in your top jacket pocket, they'll probably come out looking creased and worn. If they're in your handbag and you have to rummage around for them and pull out all sorts of other things, what sort of impression does this give?

What about the design of your card? Are you making the most of it as a promotional tool? I use both sides of my card to give information.

If you can afford a big budget, then by all means keep your card as it is and leave the back blank. However, I'd prefer to spend a little bit more on double-sided business cards than spend money on a brochure which will be out of date very soon.

You'll notice that at the very bottom of my card there's a question for people to think about after I've left them: What would you do if you knew you couldn't fail?

What does your business card say about you? Think of it as a big head-line promoting your business. When you look at your card, would you buy from you?

Not everyone wants a picture on their business card, and that's OK. But if you run a creative design company it would be nice if your card was creative. If you're a photographer, you've got a lot of scope. Remember "Kodak sells films but advertises memories." You never see Kodak selling films on adverts: they're always about memories, because that's what the films create.

I suggest that you avoid putting your qualifications on your business card. Many people's cards have loads of initials which mean nothing, except to them.

Famous Services Ltd.

John Huntley-Smythe

BA(Southampton), FRHS, MTVCC,
GCSE, GNVQ (plastering),
Full Driving License

Tel: 0800ANYTIME

You can make a joke and say, "You know, I have an MBA but it doesn't show on my business card - because my MBA stands for Massive Bank Account." People don't care what you've been, they're only interested in what you can do for them now. They're all wondering, "What's in it for me?"

Some people have a business card which is a CD that can be put into a computer. This is not as expensive as you might think. Their CD has a show-reel that shares what they do, and a price list. Once again, this is not for everyone - but if you're into IT or website design it enables you to tell people about yourself and your business using multi-media.

It's best not to give business cards out too early at a networking event. You want to make sure that your card is going to people who actually want them, either for themselves or for someone they know who may have a use for it. When people ask me for a business card, I'm almost tempted to ask them, "What are you going to do with it?"

If you ask the right questions when you're talking to people, you'll soon find out who does have a use for your card. I did a conference not long ago for school kids, and everyone wanted my business card. Now I know they wanted it because they thought I was a hero, but I've been to many events where people have asked for my card and I've thought, I wonder what they'll do with it when they get home?

90% of people collect lots of business cards but then do nothing with them. If you do want to collect business cards, make sure you have somewhere to store them. I've found a very simple method that doesn't cost much: a machine called Cardscan from Sony. When you get home you just put your business card in to be scanned directly into the computer. This is a great way to add to your records and prepare for the follow-up process (which we'll discuss in Chapter 12).

9

BE PASSIONATE!

Love life and life will love you back.
Love people and they will love you back.
Arthur Rubinstein

Energy and passion are like magnets: they will draw people to you at networking events. If people can see that it's fun to deal with you, they'll be attracted. My suggestion is that you practice in front of the mirror at home until you've got it right. Look at yourself and try out different ways of describing what it is that you do - with passion. Be enthusiastic. Get excited about what you have to share.

And at the networking event, remember what I always say:

WHEN YOU'RE IN THE ROOM, BE IN THE ROOM.

Enjoy the process of meeting new people and learning about their business. Show them that you believe in what you do, and that you're passionate about your services and the benefits they offer. Let your enthusiasm work its magic and whet people's appetite for more.

But what if you don't feel passionate? What if you don't even want to be in the room?

Tony Robbins, a great motivational speaker, says: "Fake it till you make it."

I'll share with you right now that many times I go to a networking event and I really don't feel excited about being there. I've just driven for hours, it's 7 pm and the last place I want to be is 300 miles away from my wife and kids. But from the moment that I walk into that room, I act as if I'm happy.

I often use the mantra "Fake it till you make it", and I tell myself: "This is the moment. This is not a dress rehearsal. There may be the most important new client out there."

My performance in the room is key.

More importantly, it may not be that person who'll buy my product, but someone they talk to afterwards. They may tell somebody they know, "I saw this fantastic guy Nigel who does motivational speaking. You must book him for your next conference." So the impact I make during that networking event could open any number of doors.

Very often I do a speech and someone comes up to me afterwards and says, "We really saw how passionate you are. What do you do?" And even though I'm tired, I've got to get that passion back because that's what they're buying. It's the same for you: you might be worn out after a very long journey. But if you're not passionate in those few seconds when someone sees you, they'll go to someone who is. People buy passion, not products.

If you want to be passionate even though you're tired, ask yourself:

- In the next 10 minutes, could you find a bit of passion if you really wanted to?

- If you saw a child about to go under a bus on the other side of the road, how quickly would you get there?

As soon as I ask these questions, most people find that their passion levels go up. You can always find the energy if you want it badly enough.

However, if you're totally exhausted, my suggestion is that you don't go into the meeting because it would do more harm than good. When I go out to meet people I want to make sure that I'm fresh, looking good and feeling the part.

If I'm not, then that's the impression people are going to get.

A man came up to me once and said, " I don't feel very motivated." His voice was dry, his shoulders were hunched over and I couldn't help thinking, I wonder why! His son had a problem and it was easy to see why - he was just modelling his father.

Try the mirror exercise.

Here's a tip for the times when you're feeling tired but still have to meet people. I call it the mirror exercise. Go into the cloakroom and spruce yourself up. Comb your hair. Look in the mirror and ask, "Would I buy from you?"

10
SHOW YOU CARE

**People don't care how much you know
until they know how much you care.**
Author unknown

When we're communicating with people, they need to see that we're interested in them, not just in our own products or services. It's that personal touch that counts. So when I'm networking and meeting people, I take an interest in them and what they do. I want to find ways of helping them grow their businesses and improve their lives.

One of the golden rules of networking is to give out 2 business cards: one for the person you're speaking to, and one for them to pass on to someone else who may need your services. I'll often go away from a networking event thinking, I'm not sure that I need that facility but I wonder if I know someone who may need it. You can be sure that other people are thinking along those lines as well, and if you've given them two cards instead of just one, you've made it easier for them to pass your details on.

It's all about broadening your network of contacts and potential clients. This is why I'll often ask someone for 2 of their business cards, so that I can give one to someone I know who may be able to benefit.

People appreciate it if you ask them about themselves - what they aspire to, what their dreams are, what they want to achieve in the next year. In particular, it's worth asking if there's anyone they would like to meet who would help them. Very likely you'll know somebody who knows somebody who could help them.

If you ask the right questions, you'll probably get the right answers. Just by showing that you're willing to listen, you'll often get something back in return.

So I'm always asking people, "Is there any way that I could support you in your dream?" Now I may not be able to help them directly because I'm a busy man, but I'll probably know someone who can help.

After I'd finished a speech once a young man came up to me and told me that he wanted to become a professional speaker. I suggested that he join the Professional Speakers Association. While I was happy to coach/mentor him, there came a point where he wanted to branch out and do his own thing. In order to do so he needed his own motivational tapes and books.

At this point I was happy to recommend him to the firm who do all my products and give wonderful service as well. "I speak to people about being passionate," I told him. "But if you want products that you can sell after your presentations, call Joanne Bloomfield at Bloomfield Group."

Tell the total truth faster.

Now for a word of caution. If you're not interested in the person you're talking to, don't offer to help them - they'll see right through it. Don't put a big grin on your face thinking that's the answer. A smile helps, but if you're genuinely not interested it shines through. The person will notice your body language. Your eyes may be twitching, looking around for the next person or trying to see who the next speaker is. If you're not interested, tell them this just isn't the right time and maybe there's someone else who can help them. Tell the total truth faster. If people don't sense your trust and honesty, they'll never deal with you.

I've learned to say no more often than I used to. I often tell people: "I'm really glad you've asked, but I'm not the best person to help you. It's not about you, it's about me." I am less of a dolphin than I used to be, simply because I understand myself better, and know that I can't help everyone.

If you want to understand yourself and others better, you may want to read about the Dolphin, Monkey, Lion and Elephant styles of communication in my book "It's a Zoo Around Here!"

Are you opening relationships or closing sales?

Many times you're just opening and building relationships at networking functions. That's not to say that you don't want to be closing sales, because at some point you've got to get down to business. But it's worth putting time and effort into opening and creating opportunities.

There are people I met years ago and it's just coming to fruition now. That's a long time for me, but it's worth the effort. I'll often meet people who aren't ready just then: they may have already booked their speaker for the next conference, or I may not be the right thing at that moment. In these situations, I'll just quietly keep in touch, sending them emails and articles to nurture the contact.

For instance, I've sent articles to one Chief Executive for 4 years and he's just booked me for a conference now. In all that time I didn't get much response, but I just kept on getting in touch and sending material that I thought would be of benefit to him.

I've produced some little booklets called Risner's Reminders which people can use for their team meetings. Often we'll send them out to people who have a meeting coming up, or who could use a bit of inspiration. Or we'll just email a couple of tips that will make next week's meeting better. Doing this costs me very little - just time and postage. But it's a great way to nurture new contacts and build relationships.

You can see the Risner's Reminders by logging onto my website.

11
WRITE IT DOWN

**The biggest mistake in networking is
to neglect the follow-up process.**
Nigel Risner

As soon as you can after meeting someone, write some reminders down on a piece of paper or on the back of their business card (if it's blank). Do this before you rush off to meet the next person. Have you promised to do anything - look something up, send them an article, or introduce them to someone you know? Make sure that the comments you write are detailed enough to make sense to you later. Is the person expecting you to call in a fortnight's time? Jot it down in your diary to make sure that it happens.

These notes are crucial to your follow-up strategy.

I've had some business postcards printed which are ideal in this context. Often when I've met somebody, I'll quickly write their name and address on the back of one of my postcards and put it aside until I'm back in the office. Then I can easily follow up in the next few days, as I'll explain in the next chapter. If I'm on the road for several days, I'll make sure that my postcards are already stamped so I can easily post them before I get back to my desk.

Timing is everything.

If you don't follow through within three days, statistics say you'll never do it. How many times have you said you were going to send something, or introduce someone, and days turned into weeks, weeks turned into months and then you felt too embarrassed to do anything?

If you don't make notes about following up particular conversations, you need to have a phenomenal memory. I sometimes pick up 40+ business cards at a single networking event. There's not a chance that I'm going to remember everyone, especially since most people's business cards have nothing that will make the person memorable to me. What do their cards say about them? Not much.

So how can I nurture the contact? With great difficulty, unless I've taken the time to make notes.

12

FOLLOW IT UP

In golf as in networking it's
the follow-through that counts.
Nigel Risner

If you want to build your business up by expanding your network of contacts, follow-up is key.

The business postcards I mentioned in the last chapter are an easy way to begin the follow-up process. Having written a person's name and address on one of my postcards, I can send a very quick note saying,

"Great meeting you at the XYZ event. It would be really good to meet up with you again. Let's see if we can keep in contact."

This will arrive on their desk 3 or 4 days after the event and I know from experience that they'll think, Wow! You remember our conversation!

This has taken me very little time, yet it's had quite an impact. All I've done is to quickly follow up on our meeting by getting in touch. If the person wanted something to be checked out, I've done that and told them what I found out. Or I may just have suggested that we meet for coffee next time I'm in London, or Scotland, or wherever they're based.

Develop common ground and build rapport.

I will often send people a product as a way of thanking them for inviting me to their event. This could be a sample, or an interesting article I've found on a topic that I know will appeal to them - about motivation in the workplace. For instance, I'll send it with a quick note that says, "I knew you'd be interested in this because I remember what you said in our conversation at XYZ a few days ago. This is something just for you."

You can make your follow-up even more effective. Why not take a few moments to think about how you can match what you send with the person's communication style? It's easy to recognise a variety of communication styles once you know how.

There's lots of information around, but for a quick and powerful method you might like to read my book "It's a Zoo Around Here!"

The purpose of following up is to nurture new relationships in a professional manner. I want the people I meet at networking functions to think, "That fellow Nigel is quite a neat guy. He said he would send it, and he did. He remembers what we were talking about, and he's been thinking about me."

Little actions like this can do a lot to develop common ground and build rapport. The impact on your business will be very positive. If you don't take the time to follow someone up by telephoning or sending an article or saying how good it was to meet them, how will they remember you?

This is why I make sure that I have a postcards with stamps attached so that if I'm on the road for two or three days I can just write to an organiser saying, "Thank you so much for allowing me to speak at your conference" - and they'll get the card the following day. It doesn't mean much in itself and it certainly doesn't cost much, but it shows I care.

As the saying goes, people don't care how much you know until they know how much you care. And follow-up is such a great way to show that - whether it's a small gift, an article, or a free sample that's personalised. It's really important that you personalise whatever you send so that people see that you're following them up, not just following up.

It's no different to email messages. I have a strap line at the end of my e-mails that keeps reminding people that they can look at my website. Everything is about making sure that they can contact you.

Keep records!

In order to have an effective follow-up strategy, you need to keep accurate records. If you're not keeping track of all the people you follow up, what's the point of doing it? You've got to hold on to those warm leads and nurture them, just like a baby who needs care and attention in order to grow. You've met them, they've shown some interest in what you do, and you've been in touch with them since the event. Your task now is to build the relationship by sharing information that you feel will benefit them.

Then at some stage you may need to make a decision about a cut-off point. For some people this may be after a week, a month, 6 months or a year.

I don't actually do this, though: I have an email process that allows me to follow up very easily and keep sending material to people on my list. In the messages I send I'll ask people to let me know if they wish to stop receiving mail from me. We don't want to be sending people things they don't want.

Don't worry that people will be annoyed by your follow-up. If they don't want to hear from you, they'll tell you. If you've got something of importance to share, you don't have to get a response from them to know it's important.

If an injured bird flew into your garden, what would you do? You'd try and help. Would you hope that when it was better, and you released it, you would get a note from its mother saying Thank you? No. You just did it for the sake of doing it. It's exactly the same with nurturing people. Just keep giving - if they think it's too much they'll tell you.

One last thought. Once contacts become clients, you need to keep on nurturing them. The better you look after your clients, the less networking you need to do.

13

Givers Gain

**All that we send into the lives
of others comes back into our own.**
Edwin Markham

Remember that the last four letters of NETWORK are W-O-R-K. We're not talking about netsitting or netdrinking or netplaying. Networking is a process that increases your business and will give you great benefits if you take it seriously. But if you're there just for the fun of it, you'll have a jolly time - and that's OK if that's all you want.

However, 99% of people who go to a networking event want to get something from it. If you wish to get the most out of the networking functions you go to, you need to give yourself permission to learn, to practice, to play - and to become a **GIVER** of business. When I net-work, I'm always looking to see how I can help other people's businesses.

I have two sayings that I like to remember in this context:

If you're here to contribute love, you'll find it. But if you're here to get something, you'll always be suffering because you'll never have enough.

No one ever erected a statue to a getter. It's the givers who are remembered and celebrated.

If you help enough other people to find their dreams, you'll achieve yours too. It's all about giving support, giving people leads, asking for 2 business cards so you can give one to someone else. Yes, it is tiring - but it's very worthwhile.

Of course, this approach is risky. There's always the possibility that people will take advantage of your generosity and goodwill. But do you know what? They will anyway. That's the risk you take when you choose to be open-handed. If you love people enough they might hurt you, but you still love them anyway.

I like to think of it this way. You're going to get shafted no matter what - so you might as well do what you want to do.

I've found that in general, thinking of all relationships, perhaps 3% of the people will shaft you, take the money and run, or just take whatever they can. Well, I'm happy to work with the other 97%. I think that's a pretty good statistic, don't you?

There are always a few individuals who don't want you to succeed. They have a vested interest in your life not working. Right now they may be saying to you, "This is just another one of these American touchy-feely books." Or "You don't need any new contacts, what you have now is sufficient." Be very wary of them. They are the internal terrorists, the people who drain you. Which is why I call them psychic vampires. They're the ones who'll say, "Isn't it about time you stopped writing to that person? You've been in touch 4 times and never had a reply. Don't you think it's a waste of time?"

3% of the people who read this book will find it has no significance whatever. But I've still written the book. Out of all the relationships that you cultivate, maybe 3% will not like you. But it's still worth making the investment.

With all the networking that I do, and the emails that I send, there is a tiny proportion of people who don't want to know. But the vast majority appreciate the contact.

Why let the occasional cynic put you off? In my experience, givers gain far more than they lose. I trust you'll find this too.

In this book I've given you everything you need to start gaining great results from networking. The more you practice the principles I've outlined here, the more natural they'll begin to feel. The direct result of this will be that when you meet people you'll find it easier and easier to *have them at Hello.*

USEFUL ORGANISATIONS

If you're looking for networking events in your area, you could start by contacting these organisations.

Business Link
Tel. 0845 600 9006

Business Network International
Tel. 01923 777 071

Business Referral Exchange
Tel. 01707 644 822

Business2Business
Tel. 0207 700 0008

The Chartered Institute of Marketing
Tel. 01628 427 500

Institute of Directors
Tel. 0207 839 1233

The Institute of Sales and Marketing Management
Tel. 01727 812 500

The Academy for Chief Executives
Tel. 0800 0370 250

TEC (The Executive Committee)
Tel. 01962 841188

C.I.P.D. (Chartered Institute of Personnel and Development)
Tel. 0208 971 9000

www.ecademy.com

Your local Chamber of Commerce

ABOUT NIGEL RISNER

One of Europe's leading motivational speakers, Nigel likes to challenge his audiences to think outside their comfort zones. He speaks with authority - his own life has veered perilously away from comfortable norms at times. He has learned that positive results can come from negative experiences, and that we often learn best from situations which are unfamiliar and even uncomfortable.

Having been one of the youngest CEOs of a financial services company in the City of London, Nigel knows what it takes to lead a successful business. He translates this hands-on experience into a coherent, compelling and exciting philosophy - with electrifying effect.

In 2000 Nigel was awarded The Academy for Chief Executives' highest honour when over 200 CEOs in the UK voted him Speaker of the Year.

Today he conducts more than 150 seminars and speeches a year for an enormous variety of companies and organisations in Britain and overseas.

Nigel's workshops and keynote speeches are results-oriented, challenging his listeners to expand their horizons, embrace the opportunities that await them, and dare to dream of achievements which seemed impossible before.

His range of topics includes:

- The Performance Edge - new strategies for creating personal transformations that lead to success

- The Qualities of Successful Leaders

- Mission, Vision and Values

- Failure to Implement - why some companies succeed where others fail

For more information about Nigel, his programmes and other products visit **www.nigelrisner.com**

Other Titles by Nigel Risner

"The Impact Code"

"Ten Heads are Better than One"

"It's a Zoo Around Here!" – The New Rules for Better Communication

"I want, I want...let's get!" – The New Rules for Better Goal Setting

Risner's Reminders:

10 Steps to Becoming an Effective Leader
10 Steps to Becoming Personally Empowered
10 Steps to Effective Time Management
10 Steps to Getting What you Deserve
10 Steps to Reaching Your Goals
10 Traits to Highly Successful People

Audio-visual tools for self-development

Moments of Truth set of 12 audio CDs

Self Mastery for Your Personal Success video, audio (3 cassettes for 2 CDs) and workbook

To order any of these titles or to find out more information about the complete range of services available from Nigel Risner contact us on:

Tel: +44 (0) 20 8447 1732

Email: Nigel@nigelrisner.com